Latest Will

Also by Lenore Marshall

POETRY
Other Knowledge (1928)
No Boundary (1943)

NOVELS
Only the Fear (1935)
Hall of Mirrors (1937)
The Hill is Level (1959)

SHORT STORIES
The Confrontation (1979, introduced by Alfred Kazin)

Latest Will

NEW AND SELECTED POEMS

by Lenore Marshall

W · W · NORTON & COMPANY · INC · *New York*

Note

Thanks are due to the magazines in which the following poems have appeared: "Blackout of the Dream" and "El Greco, St. Francis, and the Skull" in *Unicorn Press Folio*; "Shadow and Answer" in *War/Peace Report*; "Tree," copyright 1968 by *Harper's Magazine, Inc.*, reprinted from the August 1968 issue of *Harper's Magazine* by special permission; "Latest Will" in *The American Scholar*; "Tourist's Great Britain," copyright 1967 by *Saturday Review, Inc.*; "Dream," © 1960 by *Partisan Review*, and "All My Dear Dead," © 1962 by *Partisan Review*. Thanks are also due to the following magazines in which some of the poems have appeared: *Poetry, A Magazine of Verse, The New Republic, The New Yorker, Books, The Modern Quarterly, Scribner's, Saturday Review, Poetry Northwest*, and the anthologies *Where is Vietnam?* and *Poets for Peace*. Several of the poems have been set to music and have had concert performances, and a number of them have been read by the author for a record issued by Spoken Arts. Some of them have been read over radio stations and at various colleges and universities.

FOR JIM AGAIN

AND

LINDA, STEPHEN, LUCINDA, LAURA, ROBERT, JONATHAN H.

Contents

· *3* ·

· *4* ·

Latest Will

· 1 ·

Dream

At this waystation the ship goes through the narrows.
I have been here before. It is night.
An anchored barge appears or call it an island dock
Or bar like customs, alone forever. We edge against it,
Last stop before open sea.
Our ship must pass between locks.
I thought I would never see Far-land again. This is the last time,
I said. It is never the last.

Or never leave home again. Yet the voyage begins again.
Sprung from the deep
That fate, flat on the water like a raft,
My island, my isolate, waits.
Then carrying lanterns, single as lighthouse men,
Lighthouse turned darkhouse, quiet turned quay, men turned shadow
In silence usher us through.
O never again will I come this way
I said, This way, never again.
No more! No more!
I thought: I have been here before.

Latest Will

I, of the City and State of, do declare
This to be my Last Will.
I revoke
All prior Wills and Codicils.

Property real or personal
(Or unreal or impersonal)
Of which I may die
Seized or possessed
Anything to the contrary not-
Withstanding

In respect of securities
(Ah, security, singular, would be enough),
After aforementioned charities,
Paid to the then living issue of such grandchild
Or, if not then living, to
Per stirpes, not per capita,
If they in their absolute discretion

This ring that pressed my flesh
Indenting it with pearly heaviness
(To whom? To whom? what message will it bring?)

Also the special chain, my intricate gold, both links and clasp.
I do bequeath my fall-out shelter
Two weeks' supply of biscuits
The flask and dregs that it contains
Unto mine enemy to whom I turn the other fist.
As for my kneeling in the violet meadow
As for my breathing in the lilac row
As for my sunny brook my snowy brook my fire's glow
To one I love

Hereunder and hereabove.
First (A) I appoint and (B)
If for any reason fail or cease
(If fail in justice, if cease by inner law, I do despair)
I do decree
Which shall be included in my gross estate.
Some interests are subject to foreign death taxes.
(Are some alien interests thus free?)
All the rest, residue, and remainder, of every nature and
    kind whatsoever and wheresoever and always necessarily hereabove
(But how shall I make an inheritance of love?)
As the case may be.

All My Dear Dead

There were leopards blowing down the mountain,
I and the sky and the autumn
And the azure and the crimson;
It was a day for wonders.
There were tree crowns marching by the million
Prison walls suddenly tumbled
(I and my bleeding shadow)
Tag-ends of dreams were banished
Seraphim in branches thundered
(I carrying my loveload
I and my yesterdays)
When the whole gold presence blazed.

Then all my dear dead arose and vanished
They were free of my jailer heart,
A kite string strained, I loosed it into sun-moted heaven . . .
They were gone, they belonged to themselves, at last we had parted:
Light as milkweed silk they blew on their separate ways
(It was a day for wonders)
In the harvest flame, through the translucent haze.

At the Roots

My garden spray swings fourteen jets of crystal
Forward and backward net fanning wet beads over phlox
Over larkspur, lemon lilies; it draws a green scent from the lawn,
A swaying restorative fountain,
But an inch past its outermost drop
Dry brown grass marks the drought.

I sit in my flowery corner
In my emerald watered, watching the arch bow down
Arch and bow down in brush strokes, refresher of fortuned leaf
But falling short. I would rise,
Rush there, pour tears on the terrible scorch
Carry my garden spray where the parched lie, drag
Buckets of rivers to the rescue
But I cannot,
I sit chained to my sweet-as-rain phlox,
Tended perfume as of childhood, and when I rise I fall
And when I escape, a million wilt-free petals
Bury me O I fall
Stretched on my dampened lawn, at the roots of my moistened lilies,
        by my saved
Enslaved.

Story

From the twentieth storey window sockets
Of the house being demolished across the street
Abandoned lions and wolves stored there by a bankrupt circus
Glare down, one animal in each frame of space,
To each black hole its prisoned wolf or lion
Howls forward to escape
      (Because the circus folded
      And the building is deserted)

Deep underneath, the street
Moving with people on their way   Only I
Opposite
See
From my contrary polar window one wolf larger
Wilder shaggier press further than others   gather
His shoulders his muscles his body together,
Unable to bear it,   Over the sill,   Through the window shell
Leap   And I cannot

In horror of his crushed bones turn away
But he lands through the air on his feet
And there he is prowling immense among the crowds on the street.

Four girls in a huddle who happened to have their legs
Bound, arms bound, mouths taped, are even worse
Off than everyone else, cannot even
Scream, cannot run.

While high in the air the bellowing
Beasts glare down on their fellow.
In holes, deserted by old fires, whence one of us leapt
I and lions and wolves from the bankrupt circus wept.

Blackout of the Dream

Somebody is the murderer,
Not fate.
We who had said Megalopolis as though petting a tame tiger
Waited for the foolproof to fail. When the machinery came
To a halt the cause was a mystery.
This is the death of the american dream.
Where has it gone? Who has seen it
Stainless and bright
Reigning over millions? In one half hour maybe,
We said, all will be well, we may hope. Let us hope.
We were reduced to hope. Somebody
Is the murderer. Towers of light,
Somebody who built you forgot the sky,
Topping marvels to outwit any night infallibly
While we
Flock for an open field, press for a place
Where a brook is, a cave is,
Dark as a cemetery.

Spring Poems

The gardener dead a winter while ago
Should push at earth this season of the year
Knock clamor for admittance from below
Break ground, demand re-entry rights: I am here! I am here!
And leave nether loam for the spring of grass,
Soil, turn over; root-net, separate;
Make way, old mulch, dry compost coffin, let me pass.

My maggot fingers stroke
The sunning worm overhead;
You bursting jonquil bulb
Waiting violet sheath
Woodland wake-robin and all first green
If once you too knew death—
The dead leap from their skin.

2

Worm, sliding back into loam,
Curling soundless and pink from my trowel
Tunneling again into fresh rosebush hole
Uncovered you evade me, vanish into close-packed dark
No track where your passage stole.
Worm, moving blind from the sun
And the rose and the bright shovel,
Turning back to the black,
You can wait for me to come home.

Thoughts at Verona

The lions of the past are the cats of the present
Scampering six in procession up the steps of the empty Roman arena,
Where you sit alone, musing and rosy and cool in your youth
Augustus sat.
High behind him the arches, four remaining, upheld by today's
Broken columns,
The old stone is rosy too, cool too and enduring
Fronting new scenery on the stage, maybe for Carmen,
Arches of clapboard, half a wall painted with garlands
That will fold up and be thrown in the wings.
These veined marble slabs, these giant granite
Benches constructed for emperors
Gladiators charioteers
These sun-yellow blocks enduring have waited for you
With your gold ripple-fall of hair and your blue lighted eyes.

We are here, strange, we are relics in the archeological museum
Of a still visible amphitheatre.
Youth crumbles. Stone and love

Day by day wear away.
Or an instant's special fire of fires can powder stone
Augustus surely and cats
Break every head into less than remnants of a bust of a Roman
Or Etruscan clay shards
No incomplete circle remaining, no headless goddess
Or unsexed Dionysus. Only
You, love,
Only your youth must prevail, your musing
Hold time firm,
Renew our day.
Now hope has been given again its golden shape.
Live, live. Endure and live.
Let fire turn away.

Fragments: FROM *The Pride of Man*

1.

O, SPEW IT OUT!

That quarrel grew out of a settlement
Not bad at all; that gang meant only fun
When they began; it often goes that way.
Nobody likes such things,—they breed
Birds who fly north in winter, counter-plan,
Beetles who lie in wait, feeding on an ashy wood,
And astronauts who stay up, cannot come down.
O, spew it out! the noble pride of man,
His rights and honors, spew all excuses out.
Sir Knight, wrathful but kind at heart,
Slew   only infidels   who deserved
                                                  their
                                                       dead.

The days are fleeing and the days are fled.

2.

the trapeze is strung higher,
    that is all.
        come down from the trapeze.
           I cannot.
                now the audience loves to gasp,
                    on ladders of air
                          monkey swinging from bough to bough

. . .

the heart can bear only
    so much
it is, after all,
    a limited heart made for a certain species
isn't that true? examples of which are
    a caveman with simply a lion to face, or the horse's ancestor,
a silly Druid who could worship trees, or a Roman
    brave even far from home.

3.

AFTER THE TRIPLE MURDER OF THE BOYS

At the midsummer fair in Mississippi
Celebrants pitch their tents around the race course
Tanbark hoofmark ring-around-a-rosy sunset   Families
Clean-shirted tumbling from wellworn cars sweaty from rutted vil-
     lages
Unpack the picnic hampers
Songs drift like campfire smoke, psalms rise, the banjos strum
The way it is at the fair in Mississippi.
In the middle of the race course is a gravestone
Honoring the tomb of the neighborhood's well-known horse,
Mac Abbe, who expired in action in nineteen sixty one.
He stumbled at the beginning of the stretch
He stumbled as he picked up speed he stumbled
The whole way all the way through stumbling faster
And fast and he stumbled and fell
Dead under the rope
Setting a track record.

. . .

Also, said the reverends, let us remember
Missionaries suffering untold hardship
Who came to tame the wild Indian.

. . .

And we can always build in,
Say, Washington or Berlin,
A memorial to God.

4.

The patient helps the doctor   But
Neither will be saved.
Be brave.
          It was never a question of being brave.
That doctor's kindly psychiatric eyes
Beaming and dealing justice to suffering
Went blind. Then the devoted patient tries
To give back to him what had once been potent and sure
But
     Neither will be cured.

5.

SIR KNIGHT

God's way, which was also his, was cause enough
Since to be strong, he said, was not to weaken,
Being a gentleman he hated to seem rough
But, as he said, God's plan was greater than—

6.

GALILEO

God's power being boundless, they said to Galileo,
The universe could have been created however He saw fit.
Mysticism came easy before Galileo: Who
Can believe in the pure heart of the sun now
Having inspected it?

7.

The lady with the broken heart
Went skipping up to bed
She waved her hand, she waved her smile
What matter what she said?
So "Pleasant dreams" they called because
She wasn't really dead.

The broken heart looks quite the same
Just arteries and veins
The lady knew a thing or two
So when it came to pains
She laughed, "A skin is meant to hold
The stuff that it contains."

April Autumn

Bird on the April sill
Is it happiness makes you sing
Obeying nature?

Old man, old lost lover,
With the autumn red rose that you bring
Is it sorrow pleading in your kiss?
A chill has made you shiver
For spring's remembered jonquils
For crossroads long trodden over
For all your roads whose forward course leads backward still.

Shadow and Answer

What color is the shadow of a tree
On afternoon's cut hay field—green on yellow?
Deep over shallow? What is the sound of quiet
Bearing meadow, ghost branch, dapple? Let the world go on.
Let summer come forever, even for one,
For me or nobody, for wrens. Nobody intended to kill
Civilization: only to wound it.

Nobody said: Thou shalt not wound.
It was already wounded.
The floods were tears, the rains were always blood.
(In cave, Golgotha, and in Hiroshima)
(From claw and cross and pyre and crumb and love)
(Anywhere   Anytime)   (Look)   The wounds
Have not been stanched. Look: anywhere   anytime
What color is the shadow of a tree
What wren sings summer on a sunlit bough
What flood moves in the veins?
What blood is love?

El Greco: Saint Francis and the Skull

The drop of blood upon the wounded hand
Might have been yesterday's.

Saint Francis kneels
As though in the sombre bole of a tree,
Mouth of cave or deep of tree,
In roped and hooded robe, in spectral radiance:
And crucifix, skull, breviary.

He prays.
The symbols of his vision
Have broken forth from his brain, lie strewn; his ashen face
Is suppliant among browns and grays.
That crimson spot alone
From his pierced long-fingered clasp
Drips fresh, drips bright and now, offering
His fellow suffering
To a miniscule Christ limp on a priest's cross,
To a text and a hollowed head, a fleshless bone.

To the Sun

The blind boy said: "Darkness can be your friend
Or enemy. You have to understand it. If you destroy
Maybe you'll hurt yourself. I try to know my darkness."
It was the day
An arrow on the chart pointed: "To the sun."

The blind boy said: "A boy
Running on the path tripped me. When I picked myself up from the
    bushes
I had lost my sense of the way.
I lost all my cues. I didn't know where to turn.
I called. Nobody heard.
The worst," the blind boy said, "isn't to be blind
But to lose direction."
This was the day

A rocket turned into a planet
A planet loosed from a platform by a man
Fell upward into space
Past gravitation, racing to the sun.

The blind boy said: "You never know
Whether you are going toward good things or trouble.
Darkness is just like light. I thought
About that a lot. Nobody can look into the sun."

Tree

They were felling the dead tree. It was necessary.
On the hard ground
Men stamped and clapped for warmth.
Wind, otherwise, hurling against old rot
The winter wind at unresisting rot
Would knock the neighbor beeches headlong with it.
The man in red plaid coat secured a cable
The man, blue-hooded, hacked a deeper notch
Men stamped and clapped for warmth and tied the noose.
It was all familiar. Cold air, frozen earth,
The patch of woods, familiar, and the crack
Of axe, the buzz of saw; it was necessary.
Hacked branches lay there first. It was a cold day.
Men shouted. A woman came and stood.
It was all familiar. There was a splintering
There was a crack and crash. Men leapt and laughed,
       the woman shuddered.
There was an empty hole
Roots stiff as corpses
Sprang out, like arms and legs stiffened in the air,
And unfamiliar.

· *2* ·

Dialogue in Light Verse

Did you hear that explosion? It sounds like war.
    Don't be ridiculous; not today.
    Tomorrow conceivably, not today.
    Nobody's ready, so not today.
    Next week would be handier than today.
    You're such an alarmist about today.
Something has deafened me, what did you say?
    It's a minute to midnight. . . . . . It wasn't today.

happy, I could whistle
ill he got his anti-missile,
  I felt better when I read
    Anti-antis were ahead,
      Now I'm safe again but can't he
      Make an anti anti-anti?

I Am A

Cosmonaut
Cradled in dangers
Orbiting a garden universe
Snipping cosmos, probing Venus,
Sighting summer's end blindly,
Weightily weightless
Spinning out of reach,
            out
                of
                    reach
Signaling strangers.

Tourist's Great Britain

In Cardinal Wolsey's palace between lace curtains
Is a pink celluloid duck on the window sill.
In Sir Christopher Wren's restoration where busts of Nero
Tiberius and others garnish niches, statues of the Griffin of Wales,
Of unicorns, goats and lions line up on pedestals.

Henry the Eighth's wine cellar is not as it used to be.

If a general dies and leaves a widow,
Or someone like that, if they get on hard times they can apply, maybe,
Live here, with windows giving out on green sward, stone Romans,
In Cardinal Wolsey's palace rebuilt by Sir Christopher Wren
Where a pink celluloid duck may be seen between clean lace curtains.

Luna Sea

In the beginning God created
We who are all astronomers know
There are several theories
But later a technician on a launching
Platform loosed a moon shot from an earth
(Is there a scroll hidden in a dead sea cave telling how)

On some earth
A such-and-such ton cosmic rocket
Rocket becoming planet
Escaped from gravitation
Following its determined course in the direction of the moon.

Whose moon, poet?

The moon must be placed under jurisdiction.

Do not walk with your love under the suspect moon.

· 3 ·

Invented a Person

Invented a person named I:
Out of use and disuse
And the antique child who watched the new moon in the sky,
And a foot in the antique grave,
Out of faces cast off by mirrors eyeless under light,
Out of love and excuse

In need, on the screen of a dream:
The target of blow, the chosen of healing and love,
A marvel of fate!
Most trapped, like the wind in a trap
Sweeping forward and out, most curbed like the sea
Storming breakwater walls to the bay, like a bird that must break
       for the sky
Through all space winging straight

Longed to be:
Invented a person named I
With a place of its own
A certain thing to be done,
And in fear for that one.

Two Poems in One

1.

Being ourselves is less than love
Is fraction maimed is separate bound
The tiny pulse in thunder sound
The shaking knees on which we move
The cry shaped unconveyed by word
Our whole too half our sky too ground
All hard-won prides for which we strove
Are suppliants who long to prove
Knowing Dearest! Dearest! greater than alone.
The kiss must be given again, again
Found lost, lost found,
We are too small to utter love;
What to do with this wound?

2.

Being ourselves is more than love
What to do with this wound?
Is helpless free is singled round
By breath too own by shell too bound
Who every all and part would give
The dearest in such arms surround
Yet born alone and die alone
No other nor on dream depend
Knowing giant lift and need like inchworm forward on the ground.
The bless that in us shone
We must leave, we must leave,
Strict terrible can have
The full of reach we measure to the grave,
Only ourselves, our self made one,
Giving back to love its origin.

Unbound Space

Remember this:
                no boundary,
Space into space into space,
Islands beyond the islands that I see,
Perceived in this hour of grace
As though sight curved with the waters flowingly.

Never forget the mobile porcelain water
Leading
              and the world open and bright
As though it flew forward on blue and outspread wings.
Remember the heart lifted with delight
Having all hidden things.

Receive forever the imprint of hewn mountain
Or of lithe birch tree laced with maiden leaves
Twittering like a shower of green rain drops,
How trepidation weaves
Frail pattern:
                a virgin bewitched into a fountain.

This noon never relinquish!
                        Into the marrow
Let sink the seed of its gold, lighting the bone;
Mark how sloped rocks like flanks of elephants glow
Warmed and caressed by the invading sun;
The earth is sun beyond where my eyes follow.

The zenith moving everywhere this day
Hoard in the bones, deep in the blood collect.
Clear as I see upon the luminous clay
How moss like small jade fire runs erect,
I know a comet spinning
                    centuries away.

I know how sun pierces into the sod
Spiced and sweetening there,
Sap leaps under the bark, lilies drowse in the pod,
Barriers cease.
                Heady with topmost air
Distance circles the earth, easily as a god.

Hold this clairvoyance close, for the heart will be
            locked by ice,
The night will draw in as darkly as December,
The eyes will go blind.
                        But let the blind eyes trace
This hour still. Remember O remember
Space into unbound space.

This Twentieth-Century Mind

This twentieth-century mind
Betrayed by its own reason
Trusting in no known light
Stands in an open prison.

It has the skeptic fact
Tethered, explored, and sure,
Amended, ever intact;
It has an old desire.

Its pierced secret belief
Flowing on like a dark river,
Long ages harbored and safe,
Still seeks its own, forever.

So honeycombed by faith
But without faith in its vision
It would pray, if there were prayer,
Too wise for the heart's decision.

Asks nothing and all of fate,
Outwits itself securely:
We have found our love too late,
We have lost our love too early.

Mortality

No isle can shelter you from final grief,
No tide can bear you from the coming season;
The hieroglyphics on a winter leaf
Must reconcile you to the great unreason.

The Return

In the night, in thick dark of midnight,
Truth returns to its home,
Discards the casuist mantle,
Divests a begotten name,
Bare as at birth or at death descends to its kingdom;

Down the webbed stair into coldness
Circling and bottomless goes,
Holds to no steadying handle,
Seeks the clear pit that it knows,
Enters at last its own river, its own flowing house;

Ponders the skull and its logic
Learns from them all that they have,
Cries to the stars, and they answer
Reaching even into the grave:
"Also the heart now, Seeker. The heart can save."

Flash of Bright

Shooting star, airplane, firefly,
To eyes turned upward in the August night,
Are names to choose and flash of bright.
Which spark extinguished in the swallowing sky,
What traveler gone forever without mark
Offering an instant all he bears of light,
A million years away, a mile, or now,
Escape irrelevant where merging currents flow,
Anonymous in the clear eternal dark.

The Cricket-Watchman

All quiet quiet is the night
Closed in by stars and clover scent
The cricket makes it quieter
With the chirp chirp of light lament.

The night is empty. Giant sleep
Treads forth alone and like a mist
Erases hedge and pasture while
The cricket-watchman keeps his tryst.

What can be in the bell-clear world?
Hawks must rest and the hound as well;
Now all things cease; but the crickets' chirp
Clinks on and on like the tongue of a bell.

Interloper

All interlopers in antiquity:
Plane humming silver over ancient sky
Over everblue spring sky where
Soared the eagle's ancestor;
Smoke funneled, blacking out bright air;
And droves of ships wheeling, traffic and flotsam,
In waters newly released by the giant glacier
To nourish and harbor fishes; and gored earth strung
With wire, lacy and barbed, like a bramble patch in the sun.
Romantic, some of the old landmarks remain:
On the gray moor a buttressed windowless castle
For tourists, evening light yellows between
Fissures of ivied walls. O steel and concrete town
With the blind eyes!

Ichthyosaurus roamed the watery land
Druids once made ritual of these trees
A golden lizard crawls
On the sun and shade, on the peace, on the common grass.
Men, searching, prowling, stand
Seeing planes, a dark funnel of smoke, a derelict on the sand,
Like interlopers, self-betrayed; who would restore
Blue to the sky, clean tide to the shore.

While Reading History

Among Florentine cinquecentists taste in manuscripts,
Women, or painters' techniques was the sign;
Old masters, now, were patronized protégés then,
Recording crimson velvets.

And Barnum collected freaks in a gilded age
While buffalo were shot by great shots, hundreds in a day
Groaning monumentally over our expanding country.
Little shots gathered pottage.

We acquire,—what do we acquire now?—
Crying for one more turn, with no slogans that can catch
            an abstract meaning,
Reaching beyond our reach for the merry-go-round's gold ring,
Spending words wildly as coin, who are beggars for tomorrow.

Other Knowledge

Nothing is strange to them:
The castle on the hill
Or cabin bright and warm
The day grown to its full

Or the youthful hope achieved or the unused invisible power,
Buried, waiting to be freed,
How the mind seized slackened reins, sped forth
        according to its vow,
Or the noble difficult deed.

Dream risen on no frail dream:
How a southern sun burned
And deserts flowered and the heart opened to its name,
How peace returned.

Retrospect builds a shape
That eyes may now inspect,
The hours of life, whether in mind or in space,
Vision or retrospect.

Even the way together, classic, forever in bloom,
Is known to them moving through northern solitude and snow,
Nothing is strange to them;
Strange only that it was not so.

Question in an Oculist's Office

"Is there a lack of tears
Like powder in the eye,
Parched, impotent to moisture, stinging, dry?"

Then all the years
Broke from their sheath of shelter, giving reply,
Rushed back on an avenue that sprang open behind
And trod each forward inch again, blinking into the wind.

Things that might have been seen
Or undone or otherwise done,
Sight strained against dark, dazed by sun,
Mirages carried in vain,

These cause a certain mist
Where the way shows brimming as a river,
Wet from farewells. Gaze can never
Lose the landscape that is past,—even then not past;

So moves over the future whose promise used to burn
Like an eventual star, but now vision reaches, where
A tiger prowls through the stubble of time's square,
And turns away and knows not where to turn

Searching, peering, pressing to make its order
And by this exercise finding symptom of no dryness like powder

Only how full that light appears
With which the eyes are tasked.
"Is there a lack of tears?" he asked.

There is no lack of tears.

Love Poem

Here where you never have been you walk
Gentle and true by my side,
In a valley the mountains cherish, deep in their lock,
Where the sun falls wide.

Here where I walk alone starched juniper lace
Ripples, and there hangs the tanning tassel of corn,
Fenceless the grazing fields run into space,
Mowed sweet shock and freshness out of the earth are born.

These you would love, your absent pleasure flows
Through the empty air to the roadside, marking how
       left and right
The flying purple of wild verbena grows
Giving out light.

Filled by the colors of green, to you I turn,
The emerald of grass, the graying of sage, the dark of the pine,
Knowing how you would see this leaf or fern,
With your eyes or with mine.

New York Midnight

Nailed to the cross of sleep
To the hammer hammer lullaby
Impaled, to crash clang roar
Bound, and yet clinging, clinging to be borne thereby
Into the deep breast of the savior;
Embracing blow thong stroke
For cradle nest and rock.

Bombs fall. Wheels whirr.
A battered fort croons giant beehive hum.
Clasp dissonance, dark transport through a border,
The tumbrils over the cobbles carting
Away. Rumble long streamer of thunder.
                                    O enter!
Toss out the stone of thought
Not numb hold fast at last an unheard thing
And sink and sink toward drums of ancient echo
Past call of spheres beyond the dreaming pillow
Where waiting skies spread starless,—what remains?
A soundless sky; and still one star sings bright.
Now only love remains,
And love is left, alone,
That has taken to itself the blow, making it the own,
Soft liberation to oblivion.

Three Blocks West, on Sunday

It's not what your mother used to do
    on Sundays after the chicken and ice cream,
        staggering down desolate streets.
You're lucky to have your stuffed chicken and
    stomach and chair and that's enough,
        and no knowledge of. You're lucky maybe.
This is not what you see:
Sundays, three blocks west.

Youth with a stick of kindling playing
    baseball with thin boys, crying
        words (which we shall not print here
            or anywhere for that matter) between
condemned tenements
    (but inhabited,
        by people and rats)
           whose doors boarded up
               will make more baseball slats and firewood.
Surprisingly faces look out of missing glass:
black face (of a thin black boy watching thin white boys playing base-
    ball)
    stares from a blank black square,
        white face of woman opens at an upstairs aperture
           its mouth and calls,
and a small fluffy dog scrubbed clean
    (by someone) runs next door into empty cellar space
        beamed over by supports where a burnt-out house had been.

The barbershop has also stars-and-stripes in the showcase
 and last summer's flypaper; it isn't pretty
  but an old man
    stands, looks, and does not move from this display,
talking, talking to no one. This is the end of the city.
 Here people dwindle to no people; railroad tracks
  are last. The boys who wanted to run away
came, and some of them jumped the freights, and some of those
 (you know)—

You were well brought up by mothers; what do you see?
 What do you see from the window on peaceful Sundays,
  when you rise from newspaper sheets
and stretch (remembering the chicken) and look twenty stories to the
  street?

Why, the people look like flies!
Who could imagine it?
It's a wonderful view of the city.

Riders Against Sea

The horses arch their legs in state,
Cadenced and deliberate,
And step against the shimmering sea
Pointing their hooves with dignity.

Along the edge of wetted land
Prints trail back and cut the sand,
On the beach the horses run,
Horse and rider rise as one.

The riders bend, the horses press
Out of their mannered courtliness;
Sinews stretch and slim legs soar
Over the seaweed of the shore.

Salt in the nostrils, they pretend
They will catch the sea—they exceed the wind,
They vie with waves, close in on a quarry,
Leaving no marks on the adversary,

The ocean. Closed to any grooves,
Liquid beneath the clamp of hooves,

The innocent ocean know no race
Yet holds the riders to their place

While brittle shells are cracked in twain
And sand scatters in delicate rain.
So we would ride against untracked ocean,
So we would imitate infinite motion,

If you were here. We two would ride
Erect before the shining tide
Figures on a fresco, made
Sharp by the water's lifted blade.

Convalescent

Through window glass the stir of leaves
Silent is. Beyond the pane
Enfiltering the air like mist
Thin and tender drifts the rain.

In a translucent envelope
Sealed above the world I dwell,
Emptied of myself I wait
Chiming hollow as a bell.

Strangely remembering the abyss
(And now across the mind instead
The fine cool span of linen or
They who walk with muffled tread

Or crouched below this unrushed trance
Your ghost still lingering undestroyed),
I am unready yet to wake,
To burst the shallow opiate void,

To broach the wind or taste the fire;
Darkened, peaceful, let me be,
Fearful to regain the light
That I forsook despairingly.

Elegy to Grief

Old grief passes into quiet
Murder has been done
Breasts spell out Here Lieth
Authors sign Anon.
Now the headstone lieth
Warming in the sun.

Old grief like old joy is dead
Unhealed wounds are dust
Eyes seek focus overhead
And the sharpest thrust
Through the heart and through the head
Cradled is in rust.

Old grief dwindles to reprieve
Turns philosopher
Now forget is like forgive
Toward the murderer,
In the ransom that it gave
Its own murderer.

Two Figures

Within these figures is
The walk through April light,
Through green May lace,
Days never known claiming their own time still,
Nights claiming their embrace;
Within these figures lies
As in a Greek frieze, an Egyptian scroll, a Chinese screen,
All of another life
As though it had been.

And in them show
Magic and hope
Moulding what the heart knows
To its dear shape,
Knowledge planted so deep
Each in the other:
Holding an unspent life
Gently together.

Shell Song

Under my shell
My pearly shell
My steely shell
My crystal shell
Alone and alone
Alone I dwell.

Huddled in a head
My low-bent head
My unbowed head
In its undried blood
Listens at sound
That gives no word.

I call from within
My tunneled wall
Hearing the echo
Of my call,
Sure in the color
Of my shell

More sure of alone
And alone and still.

September Birthday

Now at the threshold of my autumn year,
Long numbers moving toward me like hosts who wring too tight a
    hand
Or like the ring of strangers' over-hospitable voices,
Standing in field where scythes have felled a floor
Blue with cut chicory layered across fullgrown grasses,
The western sky rock gray, the east a wine gold line,
I write another line as others have done before.
Old vows struggle up again toward poetry,
Blank verse were best to mark the calendar
Fending off assonance as best I can;
Notice the mind's quick tricks and kinships: "I grow old"—
Sigh at the birthright need and order the coming day.
Two hours for pen?—at least. First house, mail, market,
    news, phone, one hour
Sweet fruitless kneeling at fading flower beds,
Time out for what a budget lists as "misc."—
Items called daydreams, never planned but had,
Else where did those uncounted minutes go?
An hour to read, something to buy, a visit paid,
Always an afternoon's crusade, some fire to tend,
Dragon to slay, wound bind, and, only due and meet,
(With luck) four hours for laughter, voices, glass;
A friend, perhaps a friend, and surely love,

Armor to be re-glazed, some tryst the heart must have,—
—Look in the mirror—ah, unborn babes to rear—?—
A good soup to be stirred, a watch to wind.
This is the threshold of my autumn year
The hours ahead are squandered as those behind.
Bend, strive to lift a stone that will not be
Lifted; labor's greater now,
Breath shorter, mid breadth wider, what was I going to do?
But countering smile as swift for blue mown field,
Facing the rain gray east, light ebbing west,
Unwritten words voracious in the heart.

Forest Shadows

Here where we were young and young so often
In the dark evergreen wood
Phantoms flit out of sight out of reach, clusters of children
Long past some thicket ahead
Laugh from an overgrown glade,
Treble echoes of children, shadows of children
Fall back from beyond the next bend
Call backward lead onward as though all worlds were open
Where each tree marked another direction.

We walk on the trail of the dead
Closed on a straight leafmould aisle past reflections of
          what must be hidden,
Black doorways veering flat at our feet, surrounded by children,
Trembling lest we catch them at play, white dancing in shade;
Here: parting of branches, here was the way to their shrine
Their secret their sacred grove,—here,—one after one
          after one
The nimble sable prints fade;
Only two shadows left, lengthening, and a pair of lovers twined
Glimpsed in the pine cathedral dart of a sudden
Like deer surprised, startled as we, down an old impassable
          path in the forest pattern.

Relativity

My great stone house sways to and fro
Lightly, with all its windows lit,
Outside in wind black branches show
Bent motionless, and mock at it.

Memory, in Winter

In winter we shall not remember
Warmth of sea water; nor in summer, blue
Footprints of deer in snow;
The love that filled our other years, how shall we remember?

How trick this power from Time—
(The time for us being dead,
The fact between us fled)
To hold intact a truth no longer even dream?

Make one look substance, keep
How the heart cried out,
How joy assailed the heart,
Guard from treason the sharp original, never to escape?

Gone is the burning wish,
The never-to-be-granted,
Recalled, lying unwanted;
How give one past hour more, lest all those hours vanish?

What further word can prove
Lost laughter, yours and mine,
While airy memory steals, without a sign,
Bodiless, into the permanence of love?

Yet the scent of sea or rain
Wakes an ancient summer, as before,
Or a song, or step at the door,
Sweet still and forever, will stop the heart again.

Cure

"Surgeon, the case is strange:
Two veins from the heart,
Two blood streams bearing life
Rend me apart.

Gardener, a double crop
Strains at this single root."
        "Prune the sweet flowers
        And save the bare shoot."

Mantle for Bones

Now the soft laconic snow
Fills the hollow where it lies,
Covers root and mould and rot
Chilly in a pure disguise.

Root and mould and slug and rot
By a feather buried deep,
Who would dread eternity
Lost beneath a jeweled sleep?

When the crystal witchery
Brittly cracks and draws away
See, implacable the earth
Circles birthward to decay.

Where's a mantle for these bones?
Call back snow or summon shine—
Turn your head and dare not look—
Hasten, leaf and flower and vine.

Seascape: Ebb Tide

Between the lean land and the sky
The houses jutted forthrightly
Four or five on the edge of the hills
At independent intervals
Uplifted, salty, shingled gray,
Uncompanied by any tree,
The weathered houses sharpened
Their sides against the sky.

After the moors patched green and bald
Here in the bight lay the champing water,
Here water was watched as never
Water is watched in the open sea.
The water pulls toward shoreless space,
Hurries through arms of confining land,
Escapes in enormous sudden peace
The sapping embrace of jetty and sand.

Water capriciously stripes itself
Rough and purple, green and flat,
One water licking the other, running
Hard from the land's heart,
Breaking, running over a shelf
Where the same curled whirlpool is caught,
And out and away and into: a million-tossed
Stillness: free: eternally lost.

Inscribed Upon This Space

A stork in flight spreads frozen wings
Stretching thin legs so that a claw
Extends in spikey tongs.
Grape-blue glowing upon straw
Woven deep, immobile, fine,
The stork in permanent still flight and fear
Is surrounded by design
Continuing around a square.

The ancient Chinese rug exists
Square and patterned on the floor
With its bird in air and its
Sage harmonious character
Inscribed upon this space. The ground
Wheat colored yarn
Holds a quiet scroll around
The border like a caravan.

Here now; with darkened eyes; the fire dim;
And the door shut; we hear claws upon
Its lightly carven wooden frame:
Some monster who will break through, soon.

We had talked politics: our words
Of gun butts beating men against a wall,
Of somewhere without refuge, struck like birds
At unseen things, and of what may befall.
This momentary living in a world
Of recent dead had weighted our tongues,
Ourselves talking amid
Muzzled men and the muzzles of guns,
With our frozen eyes, in moment of hush,
Seeing black, like long funnels of air,
Hearing, clear and loud, the rising cyclone's rush,
Continuing around that square.

First of April

Never a berry
Never a fruit
This is the merry
Month of root.
Green flows up into a willow sea
And twigs take flight upon the springtime tree.

Nor blossom nor bud
Gives this perfume,
But sweet wet wood
And soft fresh loam.
Airy boughs cradle robin and linnet
And a puddle shines blue with the blue sky in it.

Biochemistry

Each little group of cells,
Called man, must face
More than this planet upon which he dwells:
The whole of boundless space.

He creeps across the sky
From star to star
Atomic matter he and they
That incandescent are.

Harvest Hill

The blackbirds and the butterflies
Sail upon motionless sky air. No rustle stirs russet of trees.
A yellow butterfly flutters up and a yellow leaf flutters down.
Time ceases, the day is forever, but the slow will plods on.
Hold, it beseeches, arresting Time; for flock and flight
Formation and hover of wing are like children playing
Their final game before the night.
Quiet has come golden. Ridges panoply
Riches overhead, the eye becomes the soul;
Halt! A long creeping toward this goal
Has labored for its heirloom harvest. Harvest, stand still.

How lovely! Why should a falling leaf, dry lace,
Drifting through boughs to its death be lovely? Grace
Note buoyed as if it had all time for descent
Tearing joy moment with such knowledge of sadness;
No shadow portends,—but it was always known there are
          last days.
Why must the dead be beautiful?

The swift blue days overtake the stubborn will
That would stay Time, clasping it right and full.
At last! Alas! cries the will

Steadfast and caught on its born course, tortoise slow.
It pursues the end, it can never have enough of the zenith,
It will shore memory against winter with shimmer and glow
Knowing there will not be another flower
Purple as this aster, nor balm mellow as this noon, nor forever
        as calm.
The will had only its goal and its hidden knowledge of sadness.
Beyond suspended day amber hoard sinks from the hill.
Zeno misled us: changeless dear golden hours
Fly like Achilles, like an arrow, never still,
Succeed and overcome themselves and the tortoise will.

Thunderstorm

Here comes the lawless rain across the sky—
Let the day halt.
The poised attentive trees relax and sigh
In shivering nostalgia for assault.

Deep iron thunders growl anathema
Lowering and warm.
Leaping in shining sheets
Downward banked lances fly and rip the storm.

Scatter in Death

When I had died I was a waterfall
Flying my flag over the jagged wall,
Unfurled I ran to meet
The precipice
With spangled waters
Silvering the abyss,
Across my plumage
Colored sunlight blew
And burred mist clung to me,
But I broke through.

I plunged forever through the waiting air,
Jetted in showers of spray love and despair,
Cascaded the passions
Pent in the skull,
Dissonant company
Channeled too full,
Scattered in death
All fury and suspense.
Fling out, bright drops,
Into inconsequence.

To a House Being Built

Each stone and cornice calls
For another definite stone or a certain angle,
The frame of the door for this lintel,
The bed of the hearth for its own
Crane and an oak-beamed mantel.
A window must hang for the view
Of appletrees cropping like sheep where the hill is long,
Porch will lead to latch,
Attic slope into rafter.
Nothing here will be wrong.
This is the architecture of question and answer;
The fated structure of deep-growing loves;
My house fulfills its own self as it moves.

Image

Over and over the moon
Flows in on the lake
See how our youth
Returns although dead

Broken silver path
For no treading
Never to ever,
An illusion.

oughts on Life After Death

Myself who like the fern am green
The fern who like myself is dust
Atom by atom join unseen.
My love transfigured out of lust
My lust created out of gland
Live out their chemic common sense
Transformed together further, and
Elude the scientific lens.

Statement on Stone

I loved and was loved. Destructions
Pounced from directions
Carried me off to their eyrie
Where beaks consumed their prey
And this became my grave.
These anagram bones that bleach
Spell: I loved and was loved. By this much forever
Out of destruction's reach.

Argument on Immortality

Though we are atoms and the self defined
As particles that add up to a whole,
Eluded still we argue on the soul,
Whether it dies, whether it lives behind,
Substantive or adjective to the discernible hand
In blow and in caress, whether the brain
Its word and its unspoken word are one;
A lively exercise; so let it stand.

But you, whose spirit is a memory
Confined by thought, impossible to prove,
Whose laugh and large compassion, strong and gay,
Perished among your ashes, you still give.
Only my animate self, though it receive,
Cannot discharge its unspent gift of love.

Respite

TO H.E.K.

Spring is your season. Where you are
You greet the newborn cherry tree,
Lids break to find the color of April air,
Wakening like wild violet, white anemone.
Now all the peace you won, the infinite breast
Is not enough to hold you from this day,
And cosmic sleep from its own rest grants rest;
The God who gave you His eternity
Gives you again your orchard; here you wander
Through quickening bark, through branching blossoming skies,
Leaving the world of essence, and I ponder
What living is when with your loving eyes
You enter in the Easter tide, and rise.

A Mother Thinks of Her Child

Over him like a tent her prayers
Hover. The salmon gives
Life for its young, but through what deeps she came,
What oceans of dark and light, she cannot give.

Thinking
       Being, of my flesh but purified,
       Being, more myself than I,
       Bright bodiment for which I strove,
       Being, in short, love.

There was an iron command:
The tender tight hand
Reaching, and the trusting eyes
In question, knowing no answer in her lies.

Thinking
       Yet must my days be dormant, tales untrue
       Until they live for you,
       No guard from any peril. Even though
       I told, you would not know.

The soft lips she would stiffen, saying, See
Such things can be.
Be spared! Here, here take of my wisdom won,
These are the very rocks I fell upon.

He will fall there too, seeing them as peaks and skies;
She cannot unmask wonder that he sees.
This is the gift she cannot give.
          Child: live.

Troop Ship

They stare into the crystal of an ocean,
Carried not forward but away,
Within each wave appears a room, a garden,
On the salt road to Africa.

Gogglehead

I was the first to see the gogglehead
Alight on a roof in shelter of chimney smoke
It was bagged in sacking and shaking a hidden shape
In shocked surveyal as if to say: So this is the world.

Materialized, perched athwart housetop: it was there;
Flapping to winds wintry across from my window,
Shrouded in caul that concealed what it was or no,
Without body, it was all head; the head had brought it from its where.

Bulged by a bishop's mitre or rhinoceros bone
Or the pronged crown of a star gone lost and blind,
Hatch of test tube or lightning, or escape of a small boy's mind,
It might be the first of legions, it might be a lone.

No angel choirs rang, it hung with never a clue
Huddling over stony street wall and inverted legged creatures
Shifting this way and that in the pit, confronted my alien features.
Poor gogglehead, I know what you see. I too.

· *4* ·

Mexican Night

On the million Mexican mountain a heartbeat under
Stars real and abstract spread to horizonless arc
See, all is visible, feel, all is wonder,
And all is one: volcanic sheer of rock
And sky and earthling merged, past end of ponder,
Whole universe revealed, apparent in white dark.

Leading the mountain gaze, drawing halt mind from its cover,
Glowing centers of space or feathered millions of sky
Open milky ways, include frail rock and seer
In silver light years, clouds of dust nebulae.
You may say: I have seen all, the reaches of bright forever.
Then ask: How stretch the mind as far as the eye?

As Though From Love

MARCEL PROUST, IN HIS LAST VOLUME

Out of the matrix
Of those lies
Light pierced as though
They had been verities.

At last O at last
Darkness grew so blind
That the heart broke:
Found egress through the mind.

Then from barren room
And bleak door
Creeping from bitter place
Sorrows turned servitor

Against whom contending
New vistas rose
As though from love, as though from hope, as though
They had been verities.

The shadowy past
Stands like a bed
Where matings were,
This seed was bred

Whose roots plunge deeply
Into grief;
Old memories
Inhabit stones with life

And make strange faces
Sudden kin,
Recovering time:
No longer now alone.

What bent key opened up
The dust?
What world retrieved
From a world lost?

The various hours
Vainly spent
Became a glass,
An instrument

Wherein to discern
What had been blank before,
The lineaments of night.
Sorrows turned servitor,

Against whom contending
Through all those lies
Light, immaculate, pierced as though
They had been verities.

Rumor

Not of new earth and not of new men
Is the rumor, is the hope,
Not of a sharper blade or clearer lens,
A serum or a law,
A steeper height to gain or deeper hollow,
Not the house where cave had been,
Nor what will ever be seen.
Not a new earth and not new men:
What do you follow, then?

For question leaps after question. The world is round.
Gravity pulls down apples, it has been found.
Fact begets stranger fact. The parachute
Descends like a homing pigeon. The telescope
Shows other stars, trained toward an absolute.
Gentlemen, the heavens have an unsuspected scope.

Searching for light uncovers further dark,
More nights revealed behind the accustomed night,
Each clearer lens and each succeeding mark
Opens new distance to the infinite.

Not in the scraps of knowledge dug
Like diamonds from the ground,

For digging deepens the obscurity,
But in the unattainable dark beyond,
Searching, there lies the key.
Oh men, for whom there is no hope,
Hope! Sharpen the blade, pursue the ultimate law,
Lie wakeful with your far divinity.
Not in the steep height gained or the lowest hollow,
Nor what will ever be seen;
Not a new earth and not new men, but a splendid rumor
Is the light you follow.

How Will You Show It

Painter, the mountain rims the mesa
Range   peak   cleft   rock   tree
Ridges unroll fierce   gentle to horizon,
How will you show it, thousand lines or three?

Mountain flames up goes out through flat of spaces
Miles   gate   arc   screen   fall
Rolls up around again, motherarms   thunderbird   wildfire,
How will you know it, circle   angle   wall?

Stare at one grain, stand before thicket
Secret of sand, sea of twisted sagebrush
Gray   blue   pearl   silver   violet,
No way to catch it all,—yet perhaps a flash?

Break the heart with joy, O tear the heart
This moment of rest
Being reborn, what you make of it,
How will you shape for others what you hold in your breast?

You are the eyes, Painter. Yours is the vision
Form   fact   passion   spirit   creed.
This is mountain or mesa. Find your religion:
The task will still be hard, but not as hard.

You, longing to share the moment
Forever to share, long in vain,
Love flowing inward, flowing outward,
But having it, even alone.